Aaaaah... MIRACLES

Also from Miracle Lab Publishing:

You Are The Sky / Color Your Way Through Big Feelings
Written by Jules' then 7-yr old son, Julian Fritz, is both a story and coloring book that offers a kid-friendly way to talk about what to do with big feelings. You are not your feelings, you are the sky!

All books available at themiraclelab.org.

Aaaaah... MIRACLES

5 Steps To Self Mastery Using

Emotional Intelligence

Jules De Jesús Fritz

MIRACLE LAB
PUBLISHING
themiraclelab.org

Copyright © 2024 by Jules De Jesús Fritz

Published and distributed in the United States by:

Miracle Lab Publishing
3573 GA-97
Camilla, GA 31730
https://themiraclelab.org

Edited by: Ruth Murphy
Design by: Josh W. Fritz, Miracle Lab
Cover Image by: Siobhan Egan, Paprika Southern

All rights reserved. No part of this book may be reproduced by any mechanical, photographic, or electronic process, or in the form of a phonographic or video recording; nor may it be stored in a retrieval system, transmitted, or otherwise be copied for public or private use-other than for "fair use" as brief quotations embodied in articles and reviews-without prior written permission of the publisher. The intent of the author is only to offer information of a general nature to help you in your quest for emotional and spiritual well-being. In the event you use any of the information in this book for yourself, which is your constitutional right, the author and the publisher assume no responsibility for your actions.

ISBN-13: 979-8-9888793-2-9 (paperback)

Table of Contents

Section I

    Overview 2

    Things To Know. 5

    Chapter 1: Mind. 18

    Chapter 2: Body. 22

    Chapter 3: Spirit. 28

    Chapter 4: You Are The Sky. 33

    Chapter 5: Spiritual Scientist. 36

Section II

    The Aaaaah Method:

        Step 1: Awareness. 40

        Step 2: Acknowledge. 41

        Step 3: Affirm. 43

        Step 4: Action. 47

        Step 5: Align. 49

        Time To Heal. 50

Section III

    Let's Do The Work Together

        Triggering Joy Exercise. 56

        The Aaaaah Method Worksheet. 59

        My Journal. 151

        Thought & Writing Prompts. 152

Dedication

To my childhood pillars... My mom, *Mamita*, you are the reason I wanted to learn to give unconditional love and patience. Thank you for the inspiration, your generous love and for always being proud of me. To my grandmother, *Lela*, for showing me how to always love and live in gratitude with big laughs and to give glory to God, no matter what. To my aunt and Godmother, *Titi Jenny*, for showing me what unconditional love felt like in human form and for sending me the strength from heaven to put all of this together and be the love, too. I love you three so deeply. As we always say, *"Con mucho mucho mucho amorrrr!"*

To my twin flame and partner in everything, Josh. A very special thank you for ALL that you did to bring this book to life and for encouraging me every step of the way. This book is for you, too. We did it babe, we did it! I love you x forever, boo.

To my beloved heartbeats that call me Mama, *Jbear* and my *twinkle sprinkles*, I leave these teachings for you. Do you know how much I love you, Julian, Jozi, and Jaiah? Words haven't been invented yet to describe how much — that's how much.

And dear reader, this book is for you. You'll see.

"Someone asked me, 'Aren't you worried about the state of the world?' I allowed myself to breathe and then I said, 'What is most important is not to allow your anxiety about what happens in the world to fill your heart. If your heart is filled with anxiety, you will get sick, and you will not be able to help."

–Thich Nhat Hanh, Peace Activist

Love from Jules

As you read, my intention is to share how I pull myself out of stressful moments—the times when life and its struggles become intensely real and overwhelming. I'm going to break down how to quiet the noise and catch a breather to figure out what to do next. With consistent practice, you'll even be able to check yourself *before* you wreck yourself, in real time.

I share teachings from *A Course in Miracles*, various spiritual texts, and teachers who resonate with me, alongside my own experiences and methods. This book serves as both an introduction to self-awareness and an invitation to delve deeper into your healing journey.

The *Aaaaah Method* began in 2019 as a five-page article titled *"Cultivating Peace in Stressful Moments"* featured in Paprika Southern Magazine. I wrote how my process was born out of necessity; I wanted to be more patient with my mom after a difficult, extended visit. A few years later she was diganosed with Alzheimer's, and now, as her full-time caregiver, I've leaned on the *Aaaaah Method* time and time again to help me find my peace. Since then, my article evolved into a series on YouTube, a step-by-step method taught at live workshops & retreats, and now in this book you're holding. Bringing this work to you from my heart has truly been a gift that keeps on giving. I am grateful!

"I'm a movement by myself, but I'm a force when we're together"

-Fabolous

Extra Love

Accountability helps you stay true to your values and yourself as you develop self-control and improve your mastery skills. You'll learn how to be there for yourself in tough situations, and having a trusted person to lean on in times of need helps.

We've created a special set of emails and a companion podcast to support you on your *Aaaaah... Miracles* journey. Head over to the website below for more support and to stay accountable.

https://iam.themiraclelab.org

Tips:

- Create a small care team of trusted loved ones that can support you in your goals.

- Make a commitment to yourself to do the worksheet pages in the back of this book, then share this commitment with a member of your care team who can check in on you daily or weekly.

- Create a code word for days you need to reach out for extra encouragement or a listening ear.

- Develop a relationship with a mental health professional and meet weekly or bi-weekly. Virtual therapy is easy to use and free for most insurance plans.

Section 1

Overview

THOUGHTS + FEELINGS = OUTCOME

With perpetual stressors unfolding in the world around us, we all encounter storms that rise up within us. As waves crash down, we may forget that we can be calm in the storm. In the isolation of our minds, wars of frantic thoughts and heightened feelings rage as we play out scenarios and attempt to predict future outcomes.

These efforts often aim to stave off further hurt, pain, and rejection. By broadening your perspective, you can tap into a deeper sense of compassion for yourself and for others, even when you don't fully understand things. From small-scale frustrations or the persistent belief that no one truly cares, I've created a method to lift you from the pit of despair and reframe your thoughts—empowering you to navigate your journey confidently and independently.

By allowing ourselves to feel the pain, we can heal the pain. Unfortunately, there's no way around it, but the good news is that we can learn to hold ourselves gently as we brave our way through to the other side... And you can do this all by yourself. I'll teach you how.

When you learn how to understand, manage, and reframe your thoughts, you feel better... And miracles will happen.

With this emergency-kit-life-saver way of being, you'll start to work with your body and mind and spirit in a clear, connected way. Imagine if you were able to identify your negative thoughts and patterns in real time and flip the script in a positive way... How much would that help you?

To show up in the emotionally charged moments and accept that what you feel are feelings, not good or bad, not even you, just feelings, gives you a more integrated way of problem solving. And let's be real, no one – including you – wins when you're operating from a reactive state.

Guiding yourself back to your center creates balance in all areas of your life with healing that flows from generation to generation. Every time you practice calming and caring for yourself, you're disrupting and breaking destructive patterns that change your legacy. This is a big deal. Gradually, new levels of patience and strength will stream from your expanding heart and impact all those around you.

One day, you'll notice that you handled a tough situation with more grace, or you were able to stop yourself from spiraling and ruminating sooner than before. There's an indescribable peace that comes from creating a life where your inner world aligns with your outer world.

You may be in this world, but you are not *of* this world.

Truth be told, I believe that you already know what you are doing. It's a matter of learning to listen and discern the truth. Remember to breathe, trust in yourself, and have faith as you release all your worries to the Source of peace.

THE NOTORIOUS G.O.D.

As we continue on, let me acknowledge that I recognize and respect all names used to point to a higher power. I use "God" as the clearest way to express my point. I want you to feel free to interchange this to whatever you feel most comfortable using. I believe the names we use are for our understanding, and Source is far greater than we can phathom let alone name. This book is inclusive. It's based on spritiuality and science, not religion.

You are whole and greater than the sum of your parts.

You are worthy of the healing available in these pages.

Allow yourself to let go... Become open and present in this moment.

Things to Know

INTRODUCTION
The Aaaaah Method

From small-scale frustrations to the unrelenting belief that no one really cares, I offer you the *Aaaaah Method*.

The *Aaaaah Method* is my process of transforming the inner storms and pain into peace and compassion for deeper healing. It's truly alchemy for your heart.

If you feel like there's got to be a better way... That there has to be more to life than what you're experiencing... You're right! And this practical method is for you.

The *Aaaaah Method* is the personal practice that I created to help me to choose love over fear every day, especially in the really tough moments when I feel lost.

It's my positive approach that helps you heal as you develop unshakable optimism through clarity. Each step builds resilience, integrity and self-trust as you repair relationships—first with yourself, then with others. No more self-sabotage, no more self-betrayal, no more projecting your unprocessed feelings on other people.

I've noticed that when we learn how to trust in ourselves and listen to the still, small voice, a whisper within us, miracles happen naturally... Even when life is really hard and everything feels out of control.

With this practice, you'll sharpen the ability to identify and release the old stories, patterns, and blocks that hold you back. You'll make room for the self-compassion and love you seek.

My unhealed pattern of reacting to life's stress was to future trip and get entangled in the what if's of what might happen. I'd rehearse scenarios in a futile attempt to damage control future problems that didn't even exist yet and never materialized. Without fail, I'd be more upset and the present moment was lost.

Looking back, I know that what I needed to do was to take a step back and hit pause, but I didn't know how. Learning to hit pause created an opportunity to tap into a deeper sense of awareness for the situation and cultivate empathy, even when I didn't fully understand things.

With the *Aaaaah Method*, I hit pause and recognize what I'm feeling by listening to the story I'm telling myself. I remind myself of my truth, move my body, then I hand over my problems to the Most High as an offering. Even with the simplest of prayers such as: *"Here, you take it,"* I am making room for the Universe to work and empower me.

I love Simon Sinek's perspective on faith — it's like being on a team with invisible teammates; you don't know who they are, but you trust they are there.

When I remember to take a breath, realize that I'm not alone and I don't have to have it all figured out. By then, I have gained enough strength to move forward. Step by step, moment by moment, breath by breath, I feel more at peace. For me, this is an unmistakable sign that what I am doing is working.

But how does it work?

By redirecting the burst of adrenaline and cortisol that comes with the fight-or-flight response to being upset, you move the big feelings out of your body into something positive. You lighten your heart's burden by training your spiritual muscles to pause, redirect the energy burst, and reframe your thoughts.

This is how you become stronger, more resilient and supernaturally empowered. You turn the dark, heavy feeling into light. I mean it, this is alchemy for your heart.

So, here is my challenge to you. Commit to taking care of yourself in your time of need. Instead of bullying, judging, or tearing yourself apart, choose to love, accept, and build yourself up in every moment. Especially the hard ones. You'll bring more miracles, joy, and peace into your life, and the ripple effect will reflect in those around you. THIS is an act of radical self-love that you deserve.

You are worthy.

I am more than enough, I am worthy!

MOTIVATIONAL FACTORS

During my time as a nutrition counselor, I learned that there was always a motivational factor that pushed that client to sit in my office to work on their health and physical body. And it was my job to remind them of that when they wanted to give up and quit.

The most powerful motivational factors included wanting to reduce or stop taking medications, feeling great in their favorite clothes again; sometimes there was an event coming up like a reunion or a wedding, and in some special cases they wanted a baby and needed to become healthier first. All different, yet important core drivers for each person.

They each had their own personal reason that reminded them of why they started and why they truly wanted, and needed, to stick to their commitment of doing the work. The motivational factor made sense to them, it excited them. Most importantly, it pushed them to keep going, even on the hard days.

Finding your personal motivational factor, your why, your thing, is a crucial step at the beginning of trying something new.

So, let's do that now...

As you read the questions, allow yourself to sit still and notice what comes to mind.

If you feel led to write at any time while reading or reflecting, turn to the back of the book and you'll find a space to journal out your thoughts and feelings.

Do you feel a deeper purpose calling you?

What dream do you have for your life?

Are you ready to listen to your intuition?

Close your eyes and ask yourself…

What do you want to do?

How do you want to be?

Note To Self

Remember... Your thing is THE thing that motivates you to go after what you want and dig into doing the work. Let's spend some time thinking about what that feels like for you. Do you want to be more calm for yourself and your family? Do you want heal old pain so you can grow and thrive? Do you have a higher calling on your heart to make an impact? Whatever your thing is, it's important.

Now, how important this is to you? Allow yourself to write a note all about how much doing your thing, your way, means to you. Speak of the honor and joy you would feel to do what you want. What does this look like in your big dreams? Focus on the excitement for your thing and why it's so important to you.

On the hard days, you can revisit this entry for a boost of inspiration and encouragement. And most importantly a reminder of your why and why you don't want to quit.

Journal pages are waiting for you in the back of this book.

ONE BLOCK AT A TIME

After thinking about what you want, the natural thing that will happen is that you'll think of reasons why you can't have what you want. This is normal.

That's your nervous system trying to keep you safe from trying something new. Especially because you really care about this and you don't want to mess it up. It's important to you. A part of you may want to keep the fantasy alive by keeping it hidden in your mind, but in reality, that's how you kill dreams.

What your dream really wants and needs is expression... A safe space filled with acceptance to grow in, similar to an incubator, for your baby dream to grow into the big dream it's meant to be.

What you carry in your heart is a divine gift which is there for a reason, and chances are you won't be able to ignore that truth for much longer. Real talk. It's in your best interest to learn how to lean in and bring your dream to life. You can do this.

FREE WRITING

Free writing is also known as automatic or spirit writing. It's a technique used to tap into your stream of divine consciousness and allow your higher wisdom to express freely through you.

In this book you're going to develop your spiritual gift of writing. This is when you write from your soul and listen to the messages that are the most important for you to know right now. I believe these inspired love notes of truth are an essential way to strengthen your spiritual muscles even more. I use free writing as a way to seek guidance; it's sweet and intimate. Writing this way builds my relationship with both myself and God.

Let the words flow freely without judgment, correction, editing, or making sense—your truth will flow out of your heart onto the page. You are safe to let it out. Do not judge or edit your words as they come out. Just write.

Use this technique to dive deeper into your heart on your motivational factor, to gain guidance, and to understand limiting beliefs that pop up along the way.

Writing prompts will help you get into the process without thinking of what to say or write.

Here are a few tips:

Always start a new entry for each writing session.

Set your intention to be open to connecting with a higher power on a deeper level.

Use a writing prompt or write anything that comes to mind, even if it seems like it's out of the blue. Set a timer for 3-5 minutes and write and keep writing until you come to a natural end. If you still need to write when the timer goes off, keep writing!

When your pen slows down, start the next sentence with a writing prompt if needed.

Reuse the same prompt as many times as needed during your writing period to get everything out -or- use the prompts given below in order.

When you're ready to move to the next prompt, feel free to start on a new page.

How to use writing prompts to uncover limiting beliefs and blocks...

Allow yourself to fully express what you want without stopping yourself. Let all of the information and wisdom flow out.

The truth of what I want is...

Look at what you've written and what you want. I'm proud of you and your willingness to be open. Be proud of you, too. Speaking what you want and identifying old beliefs around it are important keys to healing.

Let's use one or all of these prompts to find what you feel or believe right now.

The story I'm telling myself right now is...

The truth of how I'm feeling right now is...

Right now, I believe...

Find a word or sentence that captures what you feel and believe. Once you name the feeling or limiting belief, sit with what you've found.

If you feel led to continue on, use these prompts to guide you through.

I can see that the underlying fear or limiting belief is...

What I want to believe right now is...

My affirmation is...

In Section 3 of this book, you'll find prompts, blank journal pages, and worksheet pages help keep you accountable.

Your worksheet and journal pages will become a safe place to keep your findings about feelings and beliefs in one place for future reflection.

After this process give yourself compassion and be gentle with you. Do something that brings you joy and recharges your energy. Wanna go for a walk? Maybe dance and stretch? Whatever you do, please make sure you give yourself a 20-second hug. Why 20 seconds? I'll explain this more next.

A BIT ON THE BRAIN

When you are triggered or get upset in any way, your amygdala sends an alarm in your brain which floods your system with stress hormones such as adrenaline and cortisol. When this happens, you not only feel the rush of panic from the fight-or-flight-or-freeze response happening, but you also shut down the most important part of your brain.

When your command center is offline, you no longer have access to your executive functions and higher thinking. Uh oh! You lose the ability to control your emotions, make complicated or wise decisions, or think up good comebacks in the moment.

This is why continuing to argue in this state usually doesn't work out. You're in a reactive state. And no one wins when you are operating from a reactive state. Here's why building up the habit of pausing before responding, or reacting, is more important than you may have thought.

By the end of this book, you'll learn how to take steps to get your brain back online, complete the stress cycle of fight or flight, and feel relief. In the meantime, I've learned that a 20-second hug is the fastest way to end a stress cycle.

To help my kids after they get big feelings out of their bodies, we take a deep breath and hug, and as we hug, we count to twenty together. During the 20-seconds, our nervous systems start to regulate and move from fight or flight into the parasympathetic state, which calms you. You are healing yourself in that moment!

This process is beautiful and helpful for all of us, especially in the stress filled moments when you're not sure how to feel better.

Try it, give yourself a 20-second hug from me... and your future self.

Mind

After reading Brene Brown's *Atlas of the Heart*, which I call an encyclopedia for feelings, I learned that comparison is actually an emotion. This feeling drives a range of bigger feelings that affect our relationships and our self-worth.

COMPARISON IS JUDGEMENT

The tricky part with comparison is that it usually falls outside of our awareness, which means we don't even know that we're doing it. This lack of awareness can trigger us to show up in ways that are hurtful to ourselves and others.

Think about it... Have you ever found yourself comparing, and you aren't sure why or how you started comparing yourself in the first place? It's always been confusing to me why my mind goes there even though I don't try or want to compare myself.

Many social psychologists consider social comparison something that happens to us all. This helped me understand that our hardwiring makes us default to comparison automatically and subconsciously, which blew me away. How many times have you heard in the self-help world that *"Nothing happens to you, it's all happening for you."*

No matter how much you like it or not, this happens to you rather than being your choice. The good news is that even if you don't get to choose whether or not to make a comparison, you can choose whether or not to let that comparison affect your mood or perceptions.

Now, I know you're thinking, *"Yeah, Jules, that's really cool and all, but how do you choose? How?!"*

If you don't want this constant automatic ranking to negatively shape your life, your relationships, and your future, you need to stay aware enough to know when it's happening. And what emotions and judgements it's driving.

There's a choice that we all get to make. This is very exciting because when you have a choice, you're empowered. Social comparison is a situation where, yes, something is happening to you *and* you have a choice on how to respond. This is an excellent example of two things being true at the same time. Next, let's talk about how to make that choice.

TWO THOUGHT SYSTEMS: GOD OR EGO

In order to learn how to make the choice you want to make, we have to talk about two thought systems that happen within you. It comes down to God or E.G.O. I believe that love is God and God is love. Fear is the ego. Dr. Wayne Dyer breaks down ego as "*Edging God Out*," and that is the opposite of what you want to do. Plain and simple you are choosing love or fear.

CHOOSE LOVE

Every time you choose the opposite of love, you can always choose again. That's how divine Love works. You have unlimited chances to choose again. This may be hard to accept since most of us were raised to believe that once we make the wrong choice, we've messed up and that's the end of it. That is conditional love, not the unconditional Love of God.

I choose Love to get through the dark nights of the soul, to survive what Joseph Campbell calls "the abyss" in *The Hero's Journey*. I choose love because I need to be tender to myself in the moments I feel shame, embarrassment, that I'm not enough or maybe too much. That's the moment I absolutely need to choose love and be a good friend to myself because that's when I need love the most. To remember who I am at that moment is my purpose here on earth, and yours too. That's your real job... To unconditionally and radically love and accept yourself.

WHY IT HAS TO BE YOU

If I could do this work for you, it wouldn't have the same impact or power as it does when you love and affirm yourself in your toughest times. All the past versions of you, even the parts that make you cringe, still have value and deserve your love, too. This acceptance is healing.

In this present moment, you are exactly *where* you're supposed to be, right here, right now. In this present moment, you are exactly *who* you're supposed to be right here, right now. Believe. Be confident in your wholeness.

BELIEFS

In Eckhard Tolle's book, *A New Earth*, he explains that a belief, a belief system, is a set of thoughts that you regard as the absolute truth. From this place, right now, what thoughts do you regard as the absolute truth? What do you believe?

When you think about the thoughts that you regard as absolute truth, many of those beliefs were mostly likely passed down to you one way or another. You've been picking up and collecting thoughts without being aware of what you've been holding on to since you were tiny. It's a part of life and how we learn.

Thanks to neuroplasticity, our brains have the ability to change and adapt through internal rewiring, which allows the mind to grow, change, and develop new ways of thinking. The good news is that with the awareness you're gaining from this book, you'll learn how to redefine your beliefs and choose new thoughts. *New thoughts = new beliefs*.

Body

Back in 2016, I started speaking and teaching on the topic of self-care to female entrepreneurs and leaders. Personally, I knew the importance of taking care of myself first in order to be able to show up for my family, friends, community and clients the way that I wanted to show up. As you can imagine, this was a hard-sell to all the working moms in the crowd. I knew I had to say something that'd break through the limiting belief of, *"I'm not worthy or deserving to take time for myself, especially first..."* even though each and every one of them desperately needed that care.

NOURISH YOURSELF

Every time I said *"self-care"*, someone else would mention the word *"selfish"*. I decided to define and highlight the difference between the words *"selfish"* and *"self-preservation"* to show that these words were not the same.

Definition of Selfish: Showing/having only concern for yourself and not for the needs or feelings of others.

Ask yourself: *Does this sound like me and what I'm doing?*

Yeah, I didn't think so. What's really happening is self-preservation.

Definition of Self-preservation: To save one's self from harm. A natural or instinctive tendency to act to preserve one's own existence.

Yep, that sounds more like it... All you're trying to do is follow your natural instincts to help yourself. The next time you want to call yourself selfish, remind yourself that keeping you well *is* your job. You are your own advocate. You are your own caregiver. And if you aren't well, you won't be able to take care of anyone else.

BEAUTY IS SPIRITUAL

In my long time career as a celebrity makeup artist and beauty teacher, I came to understand the universal truth that your outer appearance plays an important role in your overall presence and confidence. Like it or not, how you show up matters.

In my first program with Cornell, *Women's Entrepreneurship*, there was an entire section dedicated to personal readiness. I was surprised at how much of the conversation and questions from classmates focused on how you should wear your hair and apply makeup, in addition to dressing professionally. They weren't sure what to do. But it wasn't until the end of my second program with Cornell, *Wellness Counseling*, that I had an aha moment.

I realized that beauty isn't limited to the physical body, it's how you think of yourself, your physical appearance, and your personal care routine. All point back to your relationship to Self. Once I reframed this thought, everything shifted for me. How you feel about yourself and what you look like can either be a confidence booster or become a block, hindering your power.

Beauty isn't physical... *beauty is Spiritual.*

Let's take a look at a breakthrough moment with my coaching client, Lily.

Lily is a life coach who didn't wear makeup or even moisturizer. She made no extra time for herself and believed that skipping time in the mirror was an efficient way for her to keep moving in her busy coaching practice. Even with being on Zoom most of the day, feeling and looking drained, she continued to only focus on helping others. Her belief was, *"What's the point?"*

Looking deeper, it turns out that Lily actually did care about her appearance, she just didn't know what to do. She was covering up those *"pesky dark circles"* by wearing her readers all day to hide them. She missed having the choice of whether or not to wear her glasses.

In her session with me, I gave Lily a chance to stop and

check in about her routine without judgment. She realized that she'd been missing an opportunity to empower herself, to nourish and nurture herself. Turns out Lily had been hiding and playing small, which was holding back her confidence in herself, and in her work.

Lily was missing the joy of seeing and feeling the results of her own self-love and personal care. Her hair, skin, and soul responded instantly. She had the revelation that by ignoring herself, she had been giving her power away. Not knowing a better way, she was becoming detached from her Self without realizing it.

As Maya Angelou says, *"Once you know better, do better."*

Now, Lily unapologetically pours into herself first so she can serve her family and clients with more impact and grace. She uses the care routine we created as a way to ground herself for the day, before seeing her first client. And, with the makeup tricks I taught her, Lily has the power to choose if she wants to wear her glasses or not.

Lily reframed her limiting thoughts with powerful affirmations to support her new beliefs. She now knows that her time is well spent as she honors and nourishes her holy temple, her body, along with her mind and spirit. She's healing her relationship with her Self and building her integrity. Lily's self-care is speaking love to, and honoring, her being in a language that her body can understand.

This universal lesson applies to both men and women.

BOUNDARIES

To take care of yourself, boundaries are mandatory for your self-preservation and healing. When I say setting boundaries, I don't mean building walls. It's about finding the authentic place where you can love both yourself and another person at the same time and feel peace. For me, boundaries keep me in check with myself, reminding me what's ok and not ok with me.

Maintaining healthy boundaries is key to not allowing anyone, including yourself, to push you over the line of what's healthy and best for you. I look at boundaries as the place where I can love you and me at the same time.

Fun fact: Dr. Brené Brown did some research around what makes the most peaceful people in the world peaceful. Over and over the data showed that strong personal boundaries lead to more peace.

In her book, *Atlas of the Heart*, she wrote, *"Boundaries are a prerequisite for compassion and empathy."*

I have to make sure I'm loving myself enough to take good care of me. This takes boundaries. From making sure that I get a shower when I need one or letting someone know how I feel, it's my responsibility to set and enforce the boundaries of what's good and not good for me.

This type of love and care is not only what you need, it also sends a clear message to others that they can love themselves, too. It's truly the most powerful love you can give and model to others, especially within your family and inner circle.

Here are a couple of prompts for you to reflect on. If you need room to write, take action in your journal pages in the back of this book.

THOUGHT PROMPTS

What do boundaries look like for you?

What boundaries and affirmations do you need to stop you from betraying yourself?

Spirit

A Course in Miracles, or ACIM, teaches that the Holy Spirit uses our bodies as a communication device to send important messages and information. Your body is always speaking to you and usually gets divine messages first in the form of feelings.

Science tells us that the part of our brain that feels things is not located in the same part of the brain that can articulate what we feel. This means the information usually shows up first as a feeling, and then, once calm, we have words to express what and how we feel.

Feelings are clues. Something deeper wants your attention, wants your love, wants to be healed; and the body is letting you know that you're ready. You'll pick up body clues first before you can logically understand what's happening or verbalize what you're feeling, so pay attention.

Notice how you're treating those around you. Unconscious feelings may trigger you to lash out or be impatient. You have to pause for perspective, and then ask yourself, "Why was I acting like that?" When you put words to the feelings, you can connect the dots of what is happening.

Some body clues are: feeling anxious, a tight chest, racing heart, hot and tingly in the face, you might feel warm and flush all over, have an upset stomach, maybe tense or weak, shaky muscles. You might sweat, hyperventilate, get a little lightheaded or dizzy. These are just a few ways your body may respond. In the moment, this physical change may feel like an overwhelming whirlwind of intensity. Remember to pause, breathe, and know that this too shall pass.

Your body sends you holy signals in the form of emotions and feelings. You're capable and ready to heal what's coming up. Don't ignore them, they'll just get louder and louder until you listen.

CONNECTION & PRAYER

A Course in Miracles teaches that the secret of true prayer is to forget about the things you think you need. In prayer, you overlook your specific needs as you see them, and let them go into God's hands. There, the stress, doubts, and pain become your gifts and offerings. My favorite prayer in these moments is: *"Here, you take it! Amen."*

Prayer is a stepping aside; a letting go, a quiet time of listening and loving. Prayer shouldn't be confused with supplication or begging of any kind, because this precious time is a way of remembering your holiness and reconnecting to your Source. Prayer is a song of gratitude for what you are, herein lies the power of prayer. Prayer asks nothing and receives everything.

MY PRAYER PROCESS

In my personal experience with praying, some days I need to work through what I'm feeling first before I can sing a song of thanksgiving to God. I started noticing a process that happened organically. I'll walk you through the steps that help me, but first, I want to share one of my favorite songs...

"Personal Jesus" by Depeche Mode hit the charts in 1990. I didn't really understand the lyrics, but I tried my best to sing along. It wasn't until many years later that I discovered Johnny Cash's stripped down cover that blew me away and captured how I feel about prayer, here are the lyrics to *"Personal Jesus"*...

Reach out, touch faith
Your own personal Jesus
Someone to hear your prayers
Someone who cares
Your own personal Jesus
Someone to hear your prayers
Someone who's there
Feeling unknown
And you're all alone
Flesh and bone
By the telephone
Lift up the receiver

I'll make you a believer
Take second best
Put me to the test
Things on your chest
You need to confess
I will deliver
You know I'm a forgiver
Reach out, touch faith

When I experience big feelings like anger or hurt, I allow myself to get it all out first. I pick up "the receiver" and make a prayer call. I mentally say or write out whatever needs to come out. I believe God is big enough to hold me, the big feelings and sometimes bad words, too. To me, this feels like venting or confessing the whole truth to a best friend that gets you. Once I get it out and I feel heard, I feel my heart start to soften.

I do need to add a caveat here. Venting and rumination are different. Venting gives free expression to a strong feeling, which is healthy. Rumination is dwelling in a cycle of negative thoughts. The repetitive, negative aspect of rumination can contribute to depression and anxiety which is unhealthy and can become dangerous to your wellbeing.

From there, my words begin to turn into an affirmative prayer. With boldness, I affirm the truth that I believe. I remind myself of who I am and what I want to feel. I become my own hype-man, which means I energize and encourage myself with enthusiasm and grace. Remember the grace. All of the grace.

Grace for them. Grace for me. Grace for all of it.

I offer everything that I said and felt as an offering once again. I open myself up to forgiveness, for myself and others. Forgiveness is always for us.

From this space, I naturally find myself moving into meditation. I start with noticing how I'm breathing or counting breaths. Meditation gives me an opportunity to quiet down my thoughts and listen for guidance. To be still and know.

This knowing shows up in many ways. An overall feeling of peace sets in, an inspiration comes, or even an inaudible answer on what to do next. The process of getting out how I feel, affirming myself, and then opening up to listen and feel God within me have brought me relief when I've needed it most. I give myself room to breathe and remember who I am and what I need to focus on, which is my connection to God.

My last step is to say *thank you*. I close out my prayer time by giving thanks for being connected and supported. Love is always holding us.

Reach out, touch faith.

You Are The Sky

My favorite kid's book is ***You Are The Sky: Color Your Way Through Big Feelings***, written and illustrated by my oldest son, Julian Fritz; the day after his 7th birthday.

It all started when my big brother, *Jose*, sent me this quote from Pema Chödrön, *"You are the sky and everything else is just the weather."*

The idea of being the sky helped me remember who I was… I wasn't the big storm I'd feel inside. I am the sky and everything else is just the weather.

The truth about any spiritual journey, no matter your age, is that you have to learn how to care for yourself in tough moments. You're often the only one that's there with you in those dark nights of the soul when everything feels overwhelming, and scary, and your feelings and thoughts are taking over. You have to learn how to be there for yourself. It's not always easy. It takes radical self-love, compassion and acceptance, and a whole lot of strength and courage to choose faith over fear over and over again.

I call this practice of self mastery, *spiritual fitness*.

It's important for me to teach my kids what I'm learning personally. As a family, we've been practicing ways to calm ourselves down in tough moments since my oldest was a toddler. Being open and honest about how we feel has always been essential to us.

To illustrate the idea that we are the sky, I told my kids to think of themselves as the sky, big, bright, beautiful, and expansive. Their feelings were the clouds. The clouds keep moving, and the sky remains the sky — no matter what. The Sun rises and sets, the moon rises and sets, the sky always remains the sky. At the time, Julian was six and my twin boys, the twinkles, were one. Julian's imagination grabbed hold of the idea and he started to create a story.

In Julian's story, the main character, Sky, wants to hold Grumpy Cloud in hopes of helping. But Sky becomes upset while holding on to Grumpy. Thankfully, Sky is reminded by a little birdie that we have to let feelings, and clouds, go in order to feel better.

Julian and I are your little birdies whispering the truth to you that, *"you are the sky."*

REMEMBER WHO YOU ARE & LEAN IN

To remember that you are not your feelings keeps you in alignment with who you really are. It's easy to forget that it's the indwelling Spirit that lives in you that does Divine work through you. The practice of leaning in allows you to be an open vessel for God to work with you, as you.

From that place of being, nothing can overshadow or block your connection to Source, you're clear and bright. As you walk through the chaos of life, you also carry unshakable peace and stillness within you, knowing that you are not your feelings. YOU are the sky.

It can be hard to remember who you are if you aren't sure. So... make the choice, right now; lean into Spirit. Double down on your love for God and give yourself over to the Oneness. The perfect Love of God is so safe, so warm and comforting, that you feel at peace the moment you choose it over fear. If you're still not sure of who you are, who would you be if you allowed yourself to believe you are God's and God is yours?

Affirmations:

I am a spiritual being having a human experience with God-given purpose.

I am whole, a shining reflection of God's Love.

I am the sky.

See what comes up for you by using this thought prompt:

Who am I?

Spiritual Scientist

As I start this paragraph I hear Janet, Ms. Jackson if ya' nasty, singing *"Control"* in my mind. Control is the thing we seem to be after. Control turns into a positive when used for good. Think of remote controls that drive something or how scientists who use controls in experiments, these aren't negative things. So what if we look at ourselves as scientists, spiritual scientists, working on an experiment to see what happens when we control what we can control… which is ourselves.

As you're mentally putting on your white lab coat and trying this idea on, see yourself in the role of a scientist. Reference.com says, *"...the role of a scientist involves exercising curiosity in order to ask questions and seek answers about the universe."*

Scientists also use factual judgment which is based on the data versus feelings. They don't sit around judging this or that to be good or bad; instead it's looked at as information used to find what they seek.

Now that your lab coat is on, let's put on spiritual glasses to give us eyes to see beyond judgments. There's no good or bad, it's all helpful data that will help you answer your questions. The more you exercise your curiosity, the more you'll start to understand and accept yourself.

TRIGGERING JOY

Before we dive into the *Aaaaah Method* that I've been preparing you for... I want you to grab a pen, flip to page 56, and set a timer for 3 minutes. You're going to free write a list of all of your joyful things.

Here's the twist — you can't include people or screens. Oh yes I did!

Now go trigger some joy, I'll be here when you get back.

(cue the Jeopardy musical break)

Now that you're back, how do you feel? Any surprises? What do you want to reconnect with most? Thanks to your quick list, you now have a list of things that bring you joy on the ready. I suggest putting this list where you can recall what helps you feel good easily. Boom.

Section 2

The Aaaaah Method

STEP 1: AWARENESS

Mantra: Be with me in my awareness.

Awareness is all about the real YOU, that's why it has a capital A, to remind you. This authentic, inner you is what you can call your soul, your spirit, the you that is beyond your physical body. The formless part of you that is everlasting life; infinite, indestructible, holy light.

The inner you is noticing the internal storm happening, but not trying to stop it. Instead we're going to insert a pause on the outside to slow things down on the inside. I love to put my hand on my heart and press an imaginary pause button.

Start thinking of a safe place you can go to when you hit pause. I call these places *"breathing rooms."* This will become your sacred space where you go to catch your breath.

By quietly witnessing this natural response, we allow it to exist without trying to control it. If you don't witness it, you'll blindly react to it.

An easy way to observe yourself is to imagine you're watching a movie. The little you is the actor, the big you is the one watching the movie play out. This will help to give you a little distance and perspective.

This core step is recognizing that you're upset and honoring that you are choosing to move towards peace and away from additional drama.

STEP 2: ACKNOWLEDGE

Affirmation: I am open to seeing the problem so it can be solved.

After you've noticed what you notice with Awareness, name what you're feeling. When you acknowledge the feeling, you take your power back. You *name it to tame it*. It's amazing how when you call out the fear or feeling, it's not able to run your mind in circles. Now that strong emotion is working for you by informing you.

A feelings wheel is really helpful in naming what you feel. When I have a hairball of feelings to sort out, the feelings wheel always helps give me clairty.

The Feelings Wheel

Image from Gloria Cox, The Gottman Institute

You have to acknowledge the narrative playing out in your mind. Do this by asking yourself, *"What's the story I'm telling myself? How does this story make me feel?"* These questions help you to name the feeling by figuring out what you're telling yourself.

We're really good at making ourselves upset with what we think to be true. And, let's be honest, overthinking is the art of creating problems that don't exist. This happens because the left side of our brain is trying to pull together information to build a story you can understand. All thoughts have power. They can either make a false world or lead you back to reality.

Even if the story isn't true, you can find a way to cherry-pick the information available to back up what you feel. This completely human response is called *confirmation bias*. So, pause to ask yourself, *"Is it true? Is this story I'm telling myself true?"*

Most of the time you can't know if the story is really true, so take the next best step of putting your thoughts on trial because perception is not always reality. If you're too upset and can't see other perspectives yet, go to your list of joy triggers and find a positive way to move the big energy you feel out of your body. Then, come back to name the feeling.

STEP 3: AFFIRM

Affirmation: I am choosing miracles over misery.

Before we jump into our next step, I have to add an important disclaimer about affirmations. Becoming aware of what you're telling yourself is not only normal, it's important. But your ego doesn't like change and would rather you stick with what you already know and stay in your comfort zone. This is the mind's way of trying to avoid the unknowns, even if they're positive, they're still new. Thanks, limbic system.

The limbic system is like the bouncer in a club. The bouncer's job is to bounce. The bouncer doesn't care about the club's profits or the new plans for development, all the bouncer cares about is taking out all possible threats. You gotta use the side door to get in.

You can calm the bouncer down by stepping up as the boss. You have to let the bouncer know that it's all good and you're safe. But how exactly can you do this?

You *flip the script* on negative self-talk and embrace new thoughts. You can do this by using affirmations to affirm truth starting with "I AM". Mantras, or repetitive empowering phrases, can also be helpful to express your beliefs.

The undeniable clarity and confidence that comes from using phrases like, *"I AM choosing my peace,"* and *"I AM choosing miracles over misery"* give you the extra power you need in moments of despair. This is the *"I AM factor"*; it's real and supernaturally charged.

My favorite mantras that bring me back are usually taken from my daily lessons found in *A Course in Miracles*. *"Let me not betray myself"* is a round-house-kick to all the chaos and helps me to remember that I am devoted to my practice of spiritual fitness.

Affirmations help to insert a pause to slow down knee-jerk reactions, over-analyzing and spiraling. Speaking kindly to yourself is the building block to cultivating self-compassion. Eliminate harsh judgments, especially towards yourself because your body listens to what your mind says. When creating an affirmation, I often say, it has to ring your truth bell in order for it to be powerful enough to work. Remember, you're flipping the script on the narrative.

Now you have something healthy to chew on mentally as you process the emotions. Keep affirmations short and strong so you can repeat them over and over. Believe that you're activating a hidden superpower to help you do hard things, because that's exactly what you're doing.

What happens:

Studies show that as humans we can grow and train our highly adaptable brains by changing our thoughts and hardwiring in new beliefs. Earlier, I introduced you to the idea of neuroplasticity and by choosing to repeatedly speak life into yourself, you can change your brain's pathways for good.

With focus and dedication to rewiring your brain, the new positive connections grow stronger as the old beliefs and negative self-talk eventually become weak and fade away. Self-esteem and integrity are boosted and you will begin to see yourself as more self-reliant and valuable. Kindness matters.

Next time you notice negative self-talk happening, take a minute to sit and observe what you hear. Then, pause to ask, *"Is that true?"* Taking a moment to check in with yourself breaks up the noise with a, *"Hey, wait a minute, is what I'm telling myself even true? Is it helpful?"*

The chances are that if it's not true, it's not helpful, and most likely not kind.

The next step is to tell yourself something that is true and kind. Here are some tips to try:

- Repeat a grounding mantra or affirmation to yourself internally or out loud often.

- Say a phrase that rings your truth bell and reminds you of the good work you're doing.

- "I AM" affirmations have the greatest impact: I am choosing peace, I am choosing me, I am choosing Love. The I AM factor is real.

- Mantras can be extremely useful and powerful aids in calming the storm: *Peace washes over me now.*

- Using your name in a supportive way is highly beneficial: *"You got this, Jules!"*

- If your very best friend, your favorite person in the world were dealing with the same situation, what words of wisdom would you give to them?

    My words of wisdom for this situation are…
    I affirm that I am…

STEP 4: ACTION

Mantra: Love is the way I walk with God.

In the book, *Burnout*, twin sisters and doctors, Emily and Amelia Nagoski teach us about stress cycles. Imagine an emotion to have three parts: a beginning, a middle, and an end. You're trying to get to the light at the end, but you have to make it all the way through the tunnel first.

When you get stuck in the tunnel of the emotion, that's when you burn out. Emotional exhaustion and sickness go hand-in-hand with burnout. After the surge of adrenaline and cortisol hits, clear your system and close the stress cycle by moving your body.

Emotions need motion.

Now you're going to hijack that wave of energy and redirect it into a positive action. Redirecting the energy into an action closes the stress cycle that you're in. You can't skip this step.

Here's why:

Self-care is non-negotiable because the action step is non-negotiable. The stress cycle won't end until you take action to take care of yourself. Though you may think of it as a selfish act of pampering yourself while stealing time away from the important people around you, that's not the truth.

Taking the time to close the stress cycle is why self-care isn't a *"treat yo' self"* activity. It's more of a *"be at peace with yo' self"* way of living.

Remember what you learned earlier; self-care is not selfish, it's your responsibility as your own caregiver. Studies show that those who regularly engage in self-care have a higher quality of life resulting in less stress and sickness.... Isn't that exactly what you're trying to do here?

Why yes, yes it is.

Try this:

- Pick from your *Joy Triggers* list
- Go for a walk outside
- Sing your heart out in the shower or car
- Deep clean something (ain't no clean like an angry clean!)
- Dance and stretch your body out
- Watch Steel Magnolias and allow yourself to cry
- Cook yourself a special meal
- Sit in a hot bath and soak in Epsom salts
- Do tapping with skincare and affirmations in the mirror

Disclaimer: Prayer and meditation are *not* considered an action since they don't require movement. Taking time to be in the stillness is important and it's our next step.

STEP 5: ALIGN

Mantra: I step back and let Spirit lead the way.

Here is where your hard work pays off! When you flow from Awareness — acknowledge — affirm — action, you ignite something in your soul that your mind can't understand yet. That's the sweet spot, where the miracle happens. Your choice to lean into Love aligns you with the healing that comes from the Source.

Aligning yourself with a higher power creates a compound effect of your efforts resulting in a sense of peace. This is the healing. THIS is the gift.

As you let it go in prayer and/or meditation, release the situation and all the feelings as an offering, a gift for God. Remember the simple prayer, *"Here, you take it."* Leave everything you've worked through at your inner altar, your heart space, and move into the stillness.

Meditation has many healing benefits. It reduces stress, depression, and anxiety, slows down aging and diseases, and grows your brain, to name a few. My favorite part of meditation is that I give myself a chance to connect to the Source and recharge my being. Listen and notice what comes up. Make space for God to work and for miracles to happen effortlessly.

TIME TO HEAL

Affirmation: I am whole. We are One. Thy Will be done.

Now, close out this practice by going back to the beginning. Put your hand on your heart and say *Aaaaah....* Remember you can hit the imaginary pause button anytime by putting your hand on your heart and taking a deep breath.

Next, say *"THANK YOU!"*

Claim your gift of this healing, and send out the highest vibration with praise and gratitude. Every time you use your innate power to heal by practicing your ability to calm and care for yourself, you break destructive patterns and change your legacy.

Guiding yourself back to your center creates balance in all areas of your life and brings forth generational healing. You are ending the old patterns and creating a positive legacy.

I'm here to reflect and remind you of your unquantifiable goodness. You can't shake my belief in you or change how I feel about you. And God feels the same way about you.

I see abundant blessings and miracles waiting to be recognized by you. You walk in favor. And you are not alone, we are in this together.

Amen!

"I BEHOLD THE PROOF THAT

WHAT HAS BEEN DONE

THROUGH ME HAS ENABLED

LOVE TO REPLACE FEAR,

LAUGHTER TO REPLACE TEARS,

AND ABUNDANCE TO REPLACE LOSS.

I WOULD LOOK UPON THE REAL WORLD,

AND LET IT TEACH ME

THAT MY WILL AND THE WILL OF

GOD ARE ONE."

-ACIM, WORKBOOK, LESSON 54-5, P.89

Section 3

Let's Do The Work

Now that you have an understanding of how the *Aaaaah Method* works, it's time to put it to use. I designed this book to be smaller so you can carry it with you. Use it as a journal, let it become your personal guide. Go to whatever page or section you need when you need it the most. I'm with you, you've got me in your pocket.

Included in this section:

Triggering Joy Exercise

45 days of Aaaaah Method Worksheets

Thought Prompts

Writing Prompts

Journal Pages

Exercise

Now it's time to discover what brings you joy. This list will be your go-to in stressful moments, so give this exercise your full attention.

Step 1: Set a timer for 3 minutes (feel free to go longer!)

Step 2: Free-write all the things that come into your mind when you think about joy and happiness.

Here's the catch! The activities you write **cannot** involve screens or depend on other people. These are things you do alone that evoke your inner joy.

Writing Prompt

I feel the most joyful when I am _____.

3...2...1... Go!

The Aaaaah Method
Worksheet

A: Awareness
a: acknowledge
a: affirm
a: action
a: alignment
h: healing

Put your hand on your heart and take a deep breath... This is the moment you choose to take care of you. Remember who you are and how you want to show up. You are the sky, these feelings will pass.

Turn the page to the worksheet, and one letter at a time, move through how you feel.

Compete the stress cycle to feel better.

I am aware that....
(nutshell of what you're noticing & observing)

I acknowledge that I am feeling....
(mad, sad, shame, guilt, etc.)

I affirm that I AM....
(empowering affirmation that flips the script)

___/___/___

The action I want to take is....
(walk, dance, use joyful things list)

I am aligning myself to release....
(the feeling you want to let go of)

I AM healing....
(exhale, give thanks, be still & know)

I am aware that....
(nutshell of what you're noticing & observing)

I acknowledge that I am feeling....
(mad, sad, shame, guilt, etc.)

I affirm that I AM....
(empowering affirmation that flips the script)

___ / ___ / ___

The action I want to take is....
(walk, dance, use joyful things list)

I am aligning myself to release....
(the feeling you want to let go of)

I AM healing....
(exhale, give thanks, be still & know)

I am aware that....
(nutshell of what you're noticing & observing)

I acknowledge that I am feeling....
(mad, sad, shame, guilt, etc.)

I affirm that I AM....
(empowering affirmation that flips the script)

_____ / _____ / _____

The action I want to take is....
(walk, dance, use joyful things list)

I am aligning myself to release....
(the feeling you want to let go of)

I AM healing....
(exhale, give thanks, be still & know)

I am aware that....
(nutshell of what you're noticing & observing)

I acknowledge that I am feeling....
(mad, sad, shame, guilt, etc.)

I affirm that I AM....
(empowering affirmation that flips the script)

_____ / _____ / _____

The action I want to take is....
(walk, dance, use joyful things list)

I am aligning myself to release....
(the feeling you want to let go of)

I AM healing....
(exhale, give thanks, be still & know)

I am aware that....
(nutshell of what you're noticing & observing)

I acknowledge that I am feeling....
(mad, sad, shame, guilt, etc.)

I affirm that I AM....
(empowering affirmation that flips the script)

_____ / _____ / _____

The action I want to take is....
(walk, dance, use joyful things list)

I am aligning myself to release....
(the feeling you want to let go of)

I AM healing....
(exhale, give thanks, be still & know)

I am aware that....
(nutshell of what you're noticing & observing)

I acknowledge that I am feeling....
(mad, sad, shame, guilt, etc.)

I affirm that I AM....
(empowering affirmation that flips the script)

____/____/____

The action I want to take is....
(walk, dance, use joyful things list)

I am aligning myself to release....
(the feeling you want to let go of)

I AM healing....
(exhale, give thanks, be still & know)

I am aware that....
(nutshell of what you're noticing & observing)

I acknowledge that I am feeling....
(mad, sad, shame, guilt, etc.)

I affirm that I AM....
(empowering affirmation that flips the script)

_____ / _____ / _____

The action I want to take is....
(walk, dance, use joyful things list)

I am aligning myself to release....
(the feeling you want to let go of)

I AM healing....
(exhale, give thanks, be still & know)

I am aware that....
(nutshell of what you're noticing & observing)

I acknowledge that I am feeling....
(mad, sad, shame, guilt, etc.)

I affirm that I AM....
(empowering affirmation that flips the script)

____ / ____ / ____

The action I want to take is....
(walk, dance, use joyful things list)

I am aligning myself to release....
(the feeling you want to let go of)

I AM healing....
(exhale, give thanks, be still & know)

I am aware that....
(nutshell of what you're noticing & observing)

I acknowledge that I am feeling....
(mad, sad, shame, guilt, etc.)

I affirm that I AM....
(empowering affirmation that flips the script)

_____ / _____ / _____

The action I want to take is....
(walk, dance, use joyful things list)

I am aligning myself to release....
(the feeling you want to let go of)

I AM healing....
(exhale, give thanks, be still & know)

I am aware that....
(nutshell of what you're noticing & observing)

I acknowledge that I am feeling....
(mad, sad, shame, guilt, etc.)

I affirm that I AM....
(empowering affirmation that flips the script)

_____ / _____ / _____

The action I want to take is....
(walk, dance, use joyful things list)

I am aligning myself to release....
(the feeling you want to let go of)

I AM healing....
(exhale, give thanks, be still & know)

I am aware that....
(nutshell of what you're noticing & observing)

I acknowledge that I am feeling....
(mad, sad, shame, guilt, etc.)

I affirm that I AM....
(empowering affirmation that flips the script)

_____ / _____ / _____

The action I want to take is....
(walk, dance, use joyful things list)

I am aligning myself to release....
(the feeling you want to let go of)

I AM healing....
(exhale, give thanks, be still & know)

I am aware that....
(nutshell of what you're noticing & observing)

I acknowledge that I am feeling....
(mad, sad, shame, guilt, etc.)

I affirm that I AM....
(empowering affirmation that flips the script)

____ / ____ / ____

The action I want to take is....
(walk, dance, use joyful things list)

I am aligning myself to release....
(the feeling you want to let go of)

I AM healing....
(exhale, give thanks, be still & know)

I am aware that....
(nutshell of what you're noticing & observing)

I acknowledge that I am feeling....
(mad, sad, shame, guilt, etc.)

I affirm that I AM....
(empowering affirmation that flips the script)

_____ / _____ / _____

The action I want to take is....
(walk, dance, use joyful things list)

I am aligning myself to release....
(the feeling you want to let go of)

I AM healing....
(exhale, give thanks, be still & know)

I am aware that....
(nutshell of what you're noticing & observing)

I acknowledge that I am feeling....
(mad, sad, shame, guilt, etc.)

I affirm that I AM....
(empowering affirmation that flips the script)

_____ / _____ / _____

The action I want to take is....
(walk, dance, use joyful things list)

I am aligning myself to release....
(the feeling you want to let go of)

I AM healing....
(exhale, give thanks, be still & know)

I am aware that....
(nutshell of what you're noticing & observing)

I acknowledge that I am feeling....
(mad, sad, shame, guilt, etc.)

I affirm that I AM....
(empowering affirmation that flips the script)

___ / ___ / ___

The action I want to take is....
(walk, dance, use joyful things list)

I am aligning myself to release....
(the feeling you want to let go of)

I AM healing....
(exhale, give thanks, be still & know)

I am aware that....
(nutshell of what you're noticing & observing)

I acknowledge that I am feeling....
(mad, sad, shame, guilt, etc.)

I affirm that I AM....
(empowering affirmation that flips the script)

_____ / _____ / _____

The action I want to take is....
(walk, dance, use joyful things list)

I am aligning myself to release....
(the feeling you want to let go of)

I AM healing....
(exhale, give thanks, be still & know)

I am aware that....
(nutshell of what you're noticing & observing)

I acknowledge that I am feeling....
(mad, sad, shame, guilt, etc.)

I affirm that I AM....
(empowering affirmation that flips the script)

_____ / _____ / _____

The action I want to take is....
(walk, dance, use joyful things list)

I am aligning myself to release....
(the feeling you want to let go of)

I AM healing....
(exhale, give thanks, be still & know)

I am aware that....
(nutshell of what you're noticing & observing)

I acknowledge that I am feeling....
(mad, sad, shame, guilt, etc.)

I affirm that I AM....
(empowering affirmation that flips the script)

___ / ___ / ___

The action I want to take is....
(walk, dance, use joyful things list)

I am aligning myself to release....
(the feeling you want to let go of)

I AM healing....
(exhale, give thanks, be still & know)

I am aware that....
(nutshell of what you're noticing & observing)

I acknowledge that I am feeling....
(mad, sad, shame, guilt, etc.)

I affirm that I AM....
(empowering affirmation that flips the script)

____ / ____ / ____

The action I want to take is....
(walk, dance, use joyful things list)

I am aligning myself to release....
(the feeling you want to let go of)

I AM healing....
(exhale, give thanks, be still & know)

I am aware that....
(nutshell of what you're noticing & observing)

I acknowledge that I am feeling....
(mad, sad, shame, guilt, etc.)

I affirm that I AM....
(empowering affirmation that flips the script)

_____ / _____ / _____

The action I want to take is....
(walk, dance, use joyful things list)

I am aligning myself to release....
(the feeling you want to let go of)

I AM healing....
(exhale, give thanks, be still & know)

I am aware that....
(nutshell of what you're noticing & observing)

I acknowledge that I am feeling....
(mad, sad, shame, guilt, etc.)

I affirm that I AM....
(empowering affirmation that flips the script)

_____ / _____ / _____

The action I want to take is....
(walk, dance, use joyful things list)

I am aligning myself to release....
(the feeling you want to let go of)

I AM healing....
(exhale, give thanks, be still & know)

I am aware that....
(nutshell of what you're noticing & observing)

I acknowledge that I am feeling....
(mad, sad, shame, guilt, etc.)

I affirm that I AM....
(empowering affirmation that flips the script)

_____ / _____ / _____

The action I want to take is....
(walk, dance, use joyful things list)

I am aligning myself to release....
(the feeling you want to let go of)

I AM healing....
(exhale, give thanks, be still & know)

I am aware that....
(nutshell of what you're noticing & observing)

___

I acknowledge that I am feeling....
(mad, sad, shame, guilt, etc.)

___

I affirm that I AM....
(empowering affirmation that flips the script)

___

_____ / _____ / _____

The action I want to take is....
(walk, dance, use joyful things list)

I am aligning myself to release....
(the feeling you want to let go of)

I AM healing....
(exhale, give thanks, be still & know)

I am aware that....
(nutshell of what you're noticing & observing)

I acknowledge that I am feeling....
(mad, sad, shame, guilt, etc.)

I affirm that I AM....
(empowering affirmation that flips the script)

_____ / _____ / _____

The action I want to take is....
(walk, dance, use joyful things list)

I am aligning myself to release....
(the feeling you want to let go of)

I AM healing....
(exhale, give thanks, be still & know)

I am aware that....
(nutshell of what you're noticing & observing)

I acknowledge that I am feeling....
(mad, sad, shame, guilt, etc.)

I affirm that I AM....
(empowering affirmation that flips the script)

_____ / _____ / _____

The action I want to take is....
(walk, dance, use joyful things list)

I am aligning myself to release....
(the feeling you want to let go of)

I AM healing....
(exhale, give thanks, be still & know)

I am aware that....
(nutshell of what you're noticing & observing)

I acknowledge that I am feeling....
(mad, sad, shame, guilt, etc.)

I affirm that I AM....
(empowering affirmation that flips the script)

_____ / _____ / _____

The action I want to take is....
(walk, dance, use joyful things list)

I am aligning myself to release....
(the feeling you want to let go of)

I AM healing....
(exhale, give thanks, be still & know)

I am aware that....
(nutshell of what you're noticing & observing)

I acknowledge that I am feeling....
(mad, sad, shame, guilt, etc.)

I affirm that I AM....
(empowering affirmation that flips the script)

____ / ____ / ____

The action I want to take is....
(walk, dance, use joyful things list)

I am aligning myself to release....
(the feeling you want to let go of)

I AM healing....
(exhale, give thanks, be still & know)

I am aware that....
(nutshell of what you're noticing & observing)

I acknowledge that I am feeling....
(mad, sad, shame, guilt, etc.)

I affirm that I AM....
(empowering affirmation that flips the script)

_____ / _____ / _____

The action I want to take is....
(walk, dance, use joyful things list)

I am aligning myself to release....
(the feeling you want to let go of)

I AM healing....
(exhale, give thanks, be still & know)

I am aware that....
(nutshell of what you're noticing & observing)

I acknowledge that I am feeling....
(mad, sad, shame, guilt, etc.)

I affirm that I AM....
(empowering affirmation that flips the script)

_____ / _____ / _____

The action I want to take is....
(walk, dance, use joyful things list)

I am aligning myself to release....
(the feeling you want to let go of)

I AM healing....
(exhale, give thanks, be still & know)

I am aware that....
(nutshell of what you're noticing & observing)

I acknowledge that I am feeling....
(mad, sad, shame, guilt, etc.)

I affirm that I AM....
(empowering affirmation that flips the script)

_____ / _____ / _____

The action I want to take is....
(walk, dance, use joyful things list)

I am aligning myself to release....
(the feeling you want to let go of)

I AM healing....
(exhale, give thanks, be still & know)

I am aware that....
(nutshell of what you're noticing & observing)

I acknowledge that I am feeling....
(mad, sad, shame, guilt, etc.)

I affirm that I AM....
(empowering affirmation that flips the script)

_____ / _____ / _____

The action I want to take is....
(walk, dance, use joyful things list)

I am aligning myself to release....
(the feeling you want to let go of)

I AM healing....
(exhale, give thanks, be still & know)

I am aware that....
(nutshell of what you're noticing & observing)

I acknowledge that I am feeling....
(mad, sad, shame, guilt, etc.)

I affirm that I AM....
(empowering affirmation that flips the script)

___ / ___ / ___

The action I want to take is....
(walk, dance, use joyful things list)

I am aligning myself to release....
(the feeling you want to let go of)

I AM healing....
(exhale, give thanks, be still & know)

I am aware that....
(nutshell of what you're noticing & observing)

I acknowledge that I am feeling....
(mad, sad, shame, guilt, etc.)

I affirm that I AM....
(empowering affirmation that flips the script)

____ / ____ / ____

The action I want to take is....
(walk, dance, use joyful things list)

I am aligning myself to release....
(the feeling you want to let go of)

I AM healing....
(exhale, give thanks, be still & know)

I am aware that....
(nutshell of what you're noticing & observing)

I acknowledge that I am feeling....
(mad, sad, shame, guilt, etc.)

I affirm that I AM....
(empowering affirmation that flips the script)

___ / ___ / ___

The action I want to take is....
(walk, dance, use joyful things list)

I am aligning myself to release....
(the feeling you want to let go of)

I AM healing....
(exhale, give thanks, be still & know)

I am aware that....
(nutshell of what you're noticing & observing)

I acknowledge that I am feeling....
(mad, sad, shame, guilt, etc.)

I affirm that I AM....
(empowering affirmation that flips the script)

_____ / _____ / _____

The action I want to take is....
(walk, dance, use joyful things list)

I am aligning myself to release....
(the feeling you want to let go of)

I AM healing....
(exhale, give thanks, be still & know)

I am aware that....
(nutshell of what you're noticing & observing)

I acknowledge that I am feeling....
(mad, sad, shame, guilt, etc.)

I affirm that I AM....
(empowering affirmation that flips the script)

___ / ___ / ___

The action I want to take is....
(walk, dance, use joyful things list)

I am aligning myself to release....
(the feeling you want to let go of)

I AM healing....
(exhale, give thanks, be still & know)

I am aware that....
(nutshell of what you're noticing & observing)

I acknowledge that I am feeling....
(mad, sad, shame, guilt, etc.)

I affirm that I AM....
(empowering affirmation that flips the script)

_____ / _____ / _____

The action I want to take is....
(walk, dance, use joyful things list)

I am aligning myself to release....
(the feeling you want to let go of)

I AM healing....
(exhale, give thanks, be still & know)

I am aware that....
(nutshell of what you're noticing & observing)

I acknowledge that I am feeling....
(mad, sad, shame, guilt, etc.)

I affirm that I AM....
(empowering affirmation that flips the script)

____ / ____ / ____

The action I want to take is....
(walk, dance, use joyful things list)

I am aligning myself to release....
(the feeling you want to let go of)

I AM healing....
(exhale, give thanks, be still & know)

I am aware that....
(nutshell of what you're noticing & observing)

I acknowledge that I am feeling....
(mad, sad, shame, guilt, etc.)

I affirm that I AM....
(empowering affirmation that flips the script)

_____ / _____ / _____

The action I want to take is....
(walk, dance, use joyful things list)

I am aligning myself to release....
(the feeling you want to let go of)

I AM healing....
(exhale, give thanks, be still & know)

I am aware that....
(nutshell of what you're noticing & observing)

I acknowledge that I am feeling....
(mad, sad, shame, guilt, etc.)

I affirm that I AM....
(empowering affirmation that flips the script)

_____ / _____ / _____

The action I want to take is....
(walk, dance, use joyful things list)

I am aligning myself to release....
(the feeling you want to let go of)

I AM healing....
(exhale, give thanks, be still & know)

I am aware that....
(nutshell of what you're noticing & observing)

___

I acknowledge that I am feeling....
(mad, sad, shame, guilt, etc.)

___

I affirm that I AM....
(empowering affirmation that flips the script)

_____ / _____ / _____

The action I want to take is....
(walk, dance, use joyful things list)

I am aligning myself to release....
(the feeling you want to let go of)

I AM healing....
(exhale, give thanks, be still & know)

I am aware that....
(nutshell of what you're noticing & observing)

I acknowledge that I am feeling....
(mad, sad, shame, guilt, etc.)

I affirm that I AM....
(empowering affirmation that flips the script)

_____ / _____ / _____

The action I want to take is....
(walk, dance, use joyful things list)

I am aligning myself to release....
(the feeling you want to let go of)

I AM healing....
(exhale, give thanks, be still & know)

I am aware that....
(nutshell of what you're noticing & observing)

I acknowledge that I am feeling....
(mad, sad, shame, guilt, etc.)

I affirm that I AM....
(empowering affirmation that flips the script)

____/____/____

The action I want to take is....
(walk, dance, use joyful things list)

I am aligning myself to release....
(the feeling you want to let go of)

I AM healing....
(exhale, give thanks, be still & know)

I am aware that....
(nutshell of what you're noticing & observing)

I acknowledge that I am feeling....
(mad, sad, shame, guilt, etc.)

I affirm that I AM....
(empowering affirmation that flips the script)

_____ / _____ / _____

The action I want to take is....
(walk, dance, use joyful things list)

I am aligning myself to release....
(the feeling you want to let go of)

I AM healing....
(exhale, give thanks, be still & know)

I am aware that....
(nutshell of what you're noticing & observing)

I acknowledge that I am feeling....
(mad, sad, shame, guilt, etc.)

I affirm that I AM....
(empowering affirmation that flips the script)

_____ / _____ / _____

The action I want to take is....
(walk, dance, use joyful things list)

I am aligning myself to release....
(the feeling you want to let go of)

I AM healing....
(exhale, give thanks, be still & know)

My Journal

Studies show that writing in a journal benefits your mental and physical health. It improves your memory and insights while also fostering original thinking. Writing allows us to think freely and safely discover new ideas, perspectives, and beliefs, unlocking our full potential.

In addtion to the break down on free writing, I've listed out prompts to help get you going. Use them however you want.

This next section is all for you.

Allow yourself to let go and flow.

You are more than enough, you are worthy.

And you got this. xo

Thought Prompts

Do you feel a deeper purpose calling you?

What dream do you have for your life?

Are you ready to listen to your intuition?

Close your eyes and ask yourself…

What do you want to do?

How do you want to be?

What do boundaries look like for you?

What boundaries and affirmations do you need to stop you from betraying yourself?

If your very best friend, your favorite person in the world were dealing with the same situation, what words of wisdom would you give to them?

Writing Prompts

The truth of what I want is…

The story I'm telling myself right now is…

The truth of how I'm feeling right now is…

Right now, I believe…

I can see that the underlying fear or limiting belief is…

What I want to believe right now is…

The thoughts I regard as the absolute truth are…

My affirmation is…

My words of wisdom for this situation are…

I affirm that I am…

Freewrite

Let it flow

Freewrite

Let it flow

Freewrite

Let it flow

Freewrite

Let it Flow

Freewrite

Let it flow

Freewrite

Let it flow

Freewrite

Let it flow

Freewrite

Let it flow

Freewrite

Let it flow

Freewrite

Let it flow

Freewrite

Let it flow

Freewrite

Let it Flow

About the author

Jules De Jesús Fritz
Spiritual Wellness Coach

Jules surrendered her career as a celebrity makeup artist to take a leap of faith and follow a higher calling. She traveled the country for 2 years with her husband and young son in a vintage Airstream named Lovie. In that time Jules dug into her own healing to uncover her inner purpose and became trained to confidentially and responsibly hold space. She served as a Unity prayer chaplain and graduated from both the Wellness Counseling & Women's Entrepreneurship programs with Cornell University, focusing on wellness for organizations and entreprenuers.

Jules then became a co-creator of Miracle Lab with her husband, Josh. This dynamic duo uses their unique skills to bring clients clarity and impact; by aligning their vision, mission, and beliefs with online outreach. Through coaching, workshops, and retreats, their clients are able to find their peace, feel the freedom they seek, and create the impact they desire.

Jules and Josh still love to travel and are based on their 25-acre homestead in Hopeful, GA. They homeschool their boys Julian and twins, Jozi and Jaiah, and are caregivers to Jules' mom who is thriving even with advanced stage Alzheimer's disease. They're all grateful to live this full and beautiful life together.

Work with Jules

Speaking Engagements

Live Workshops & On-Demand Trainings

Retreat Facilitator

Life & Business Coaching

Connect

Email: hello@themiraclelab.org

Visit Us Online: https://themiraclelab.org

YouTube/Instagram: @miraclelab1111

LinkedIn: @julesdejesusfritz

Made in the USA
Middletown, DE
19 October 2024